ANCIENT
EGYPT

ANCIENT CIVILIZATIONS

ANCIENT
EGYPT

Edited by Sherman Hollar

Britannica
Educational Publishing

IN ASSOCIATION WITH

ROSEN
EDUCATIONAL SERVICES

Published in 2012 by Britannica Educational Publishing
(a trademark of Encyclopædia Britannica, Inc.)
in association with Rosen Educational Services, LLC
29 East 21st Street, New York, NY 10010.

Distributed exclusively by Rosen Educational Services.
For a listing of additional Britannica Educational Publishing titles, call toll free (800) 237-9932.

First Edition

Britannica Educational Publishing
Michael I. Levy: Executive Editor, Encyclopædia Britannica
J.E. Luebering: Director, Core Reference Group, Encyclopædia Britannica
Adam Augustyn: Assistant Manager, Encyclopædia Britannica

Anthony L. Green: Editor, Compton's by Britannica
Michael Anderson: Senior Editor, Compton's by Britannica
Sherman Hollar: Associate Editor, Compton's by Britannica

Marilyn L. Barton: Senior Coordinator, Production Control
Steven Bosco: Director, Editorial Technologies
Lisa S. Braucher: Senior Producer and Data Editor
Yvette Charboneau: Senior Copy Editor
Kathy Nakamura: Manager, Media Acquisition

Rosen Educational Services
Alexandra Hanson-Harding: Editor
Nelson Sá: Art Director
Cindy Reiman: Photography Manager
Matthew Cauli: Designer, Cover Design
Introduction by Alexandra Hanson-Harding

Library of Congress Cataloging-in-Publication Data

Ancient Egypt / edited by Sherman Hollar.—1st ed.
    p. cm.—(Ancient civilizations)
"In association with Britannica Educational Publishing, Rosen Educational Services."
Includes bibliographical references and index.
ISBN 978-1-61530-523-0 (library binding)
1. Egypt—Civilization—To 332 B.C.—Juvenile literature. 2. Egypt—History—To 332 B.C.—Juvenile
literature. I. Hollar, Sherman. II. Series: Ancient civilizations (Britannica Educational Publishing)
DT61.A593 2012
932'.01—dc22

                                                                                        2011004714

Manufactured in the United States of America

On the cover, page 3: Pyramids in Egypt's Giza valley under sunset light. *Shutterstock.com*

Pages 10, 28, 46, 58, 75 © www.istockphoto.com/Tat Mun Lui; pp. 13,14, 15, 32, 33, 34, 43, 44, 45, 50, 51, 54,
55, 59, 60, 71, 72 © www.istockphoto.com/Vasko Miokovic Photography; remaining interior background
image © www.istockphoto.com/sculpies; back cover Shutterstock.com

CONTENTS

The sands of the Sahara Desert might not seem a likely home for one of the world's greatest empires. But the Nile River made the Egyptian empire possible. The Nile is a lifeline winding north from Ethiopia's highland through Egypt to drain into the Mediterranean Sea. The Egyptians could grow plentiful crops because each year the river flooded, bringing dark, silty soil. Learning how to manage the flooding and then to reclaim and irrigate the land helped the Egyptians develop into a coherent society. As the ancient Greek historian Herodotus said, "Egypt is the gift of the Nile."

The Nile—and its location—helped Egyptian civilization to last, in a relatively unchanged form, for more than 3,000 years. During that same time, mighty empires had risen and fallen in Mesopotamia and other less protected places. But hemmed in by the forbidding desert, Egypt was, aside from the trade it carried on, mostly a world apart.

In this volume you will learn how, in prehistoric times, the Egyptians changed from being hunters and gatherers to farmers and craftsmen. As the climate gradually became drier, cooperation helped the early Egyptians to form villages, then cities. In approximately

This massive statue shows Ramses II, one of Egypt's most famous pharaohs.
Shutterstock.com

3000 BC—when written records started being kept—the legendary King Menes brought Upper (southern) and Lower (northern) Egypt together to form a single nation. Egypt's three most powerful periods of the historical era are called the Old Kingdom, Middle Kingdom, and New Kingdom. It was during the Old Kingdom that the great pyramids were built.

Over time, Egypt gradually weakened and became vulnerable to foreign invaders, such as the Assyrians, the Kushites, and the Greeks. Finally, despite the efforts of Egypt's last ruler, the wily Cleopatra, the powerful Roman Empire took over in 31 BC.

Upper class Egyptians had elegant lives. They wore simple linen sheaths, but for special occasions, both men and women wore jewelry, used perfume and makeup, and wore elaborate wigs. They had relatively little furniture, but what they did have was sophisticated and made of fine materials. Farmers had a harder time. They were not only taxed heavily, but they could also be called upon to work on giant public work projects. Some of these were grand stone temples to honor their gods. Other extravagant structures were gigantic tombs for the pharaohs.

The Egyptians loved life and were hopeful that their souls would be reunited with their bodies after death. This hopefulness, combined with the fact that bodies could stay well-preserved in the dry atmosphere, led to the practice of mummification. Not only were humans given this elaborate preservation treatment, but so were certain animals, including cats, which were considered sacred by the Egyptians.

From studying their tombs and other ancient buildings, we have learned much about Egypt's culture. Their art represented ideas of Egyptian society—for example, a servant might appear smaller than a lord. Images, often painted on tomb walls as fresco, showed all kinds of scenes of Egyptian life—from queens communing with goddesses to farmers cutting grain or waterbirds flying over marshes. We have also learned about their three different types of writing, including hieroglyphics, the beautiful, stylized picture language. They wrote on paper made from the papyrus plant.

Ancient Egypt is long gone, but the civilization remains a source of fascination. Its long, stable history, refined art, and vast engineering accomplishments hint at a way of life that is both familiar and very different from our own and continues to inspire creativity today.

CHAPTER 1

THE WORLD OF THE ANCIENT EGYPTIANS

No other country—not even China or India—has such a long unbroken history as Egypt. Nearly 3,000 years before the birth of Jesus, the Egyptians had reached a high stage of civilization. They lived under an orderly government; they carried on commerce in ships; they built great stone structures; and, most important of all, they had acquired the art of writing. In the Nile River Valley, where the Egyptian people lived, the early development of the arts and crafts that formed the foundation of Western civilization can be traced.

The traveler along the Nile sees many majestic monuments that reveal the achievements of ancient Egypt. Most of these monuments are tombs and temples. The ancient Egyptians were very religious. They believed in a life after death—at first only for kings and nobles—if the body could be preserved. So they carefully embalmed the body and walled it up in a massive tomb. On the walls of the tomb they carved pictures

Egyptian dancing, detail from a tomb painting from Shaykh 'Abd al-Qurnah, Egypt, c. 1400 BC; in the British Museum, London. **Courtesy of the trustees of the British Museum**

and inscriptions. Some private tombs were decorated with paintings. They put into the tomb the person's statue and any objects they thought would be needed when the soul returned to the body. The hot sand and dry air of Egypt preserved many of these objects through the centuries. Thousands of them are now in museums all over the world. Together with written documents, they show how people lived in ancient Egypt.

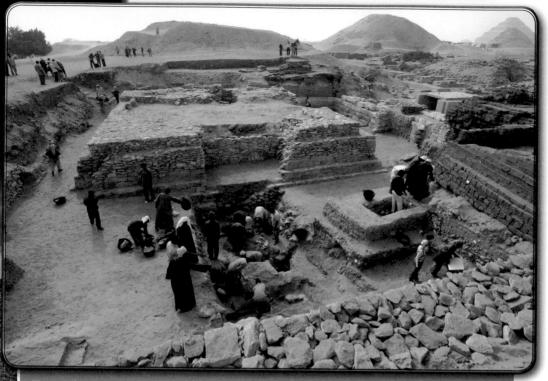

Egyptian archaeologists work at an ancient burial ground in Saqqara, Egypt. The 4,300-year-old pyramid of Queen Sesheshet, the mother of King Teti, founder of Egypt's 6th dynasty, was discovered here. **Khaled Desouki/AFP/Getty Images**

The desert sands have also preserved the remains of prehistoric people. By their sides, in the burial pits, lie stone tools and weapons, carved figures, and decorated pottery. These artifacts help archaeologists and historians piece together the story of life in the Nile Valley centuries before the beginning of the historical period.

THE ART OF MUMMIFICATION

In the great museum of Egyptian antiquities in Cairo, throngs of sightseers daily look into the very faces of the pharaohs and nobles who ruled Egypt many centuries ago. They were preserved as mummies, thousands of which have been taken from the sands and tombs of Egypt. The word *mummy* refers to a dead body in which some of the soft tissue has been preserved along with the bones. The Egyptians practiced the art of mummifying their dead for 3,000 years or more in the belief that the soul would be reunited with the body in the afterlife, so the body had to be kept intact. The most carefully prepared Egyptian mummies date from about 1000 BC, but the earliest ones discovered are much older. Sacred animals, such as cats, ibises, and crocodiles, were also mummified.

The most elaborate Egyptian process, used for royalty and the wealthy, took about 70 days. First, most of the internal organs were removed. The brain was usually extracted through the nostrils with a hook and then discarded. The heart, considered the most important organ, was usually left in place. Most of the other vital organs were embalmed and placed in four vessels, called canopic jars, which were buried with the body. (In later Egyptian times, the treated organs were

A wooden coffin lies open showing the mummy inside at an excavation site in Saqqara, Egypt. Archaeologists discovered three ancient coffins dating back to the 26th pharaonic dynasty, which ruled from 672 BC to 525 BC. **AFP/Getty Images**

returned to the body cavity rather than sealed in jars.) The body was washed with palm wine (which would have helped kill bacteria) and then covered with natron, a salt, and left for many days to thoroughly dry out. Next, the body was treated with resin, oils, spices, palm wine, and other substances to help preserve it. It was then wrapped in strips of linen.

The shrouded mummy was usually placed in two cases of cedar or of cloth stiffened with glue. The outer case was often covered with paintings and hieroglyphics telling of the life of the deceased. A molded mask of the dead or a portrait on linen or wood sometimes decorated the head end of the case. This double case was placed in an oblong coffin and deposited in a sarcophagus.

THE NILE

To understand how Egypt developed into a great civilization, it is first important to understand its setting. Though most of Egypt's land is made up of the forbidding Sahara Desert, the Nile River snakes through this land as a vital lifeline. The Nile is the longest river in the world. It rises south of the equator and flows northward through northeastern Africa to drain into the Mediterranean Sea. It has a length of about 4,132 miles (6,650 kilometers) and drains an area estimated at 1,293,000 square miles (3,349,000 square kilometers). The Nile River basin covers about one-tenth of the area of the continent.

The Nile is formed by three principal streams, the Blue Nile and the Atbara, which flow from the highlands of Ethiopia, and the White Nile, the headstreams of which flow into Lakes Victoria and Albert.

In Egypt, the availability of water from the Nile throughout the year, combined with the area's high temperatures, makes possible intensive cultivation along its banks. Also important are the rich, fertile sediments the river carries when it is in flood and leaves on the river's banks. This rich mud is so dark that Egyptians first called the land Kem or Kemi, which means "black." The Nile River is also a vital waterway for transport.

The Nile swells in the summer, the floods rising as a result of the heavy tropical rains in the highlands of Ethiopia. The effect is not felt at southern Aswan, Egypt, until July. The water then starts to rise and continues to do so throughout August and September, with the maximum occurring in mid-September. At Cairo, farther north, the maximum is delayed until October. The level of the river then falls rapidly through November and December. From March to May the level of the river is at its lowest. Although the flood is a fairly regular phenomenon, it occasionally varies in volume and date. Before dams made it possible to

Traditional vessel called a faluka *sailing on the* *Nile.* **Jack Guez/AFP/Getty Images**

regulate the river in modern times, years of high or low flood—particularly a sequence of such years—resulted in crop failure, famine, and disease.

North of Cairo the Nile enters the delta region, a level, triangular-shaped lowland. The Nile delta comprises a gulf of the prehistoric Mediterranean Sea that has been filled in; it is composed of silt brought mainly from the Ethiopian Plateau. The silt varies in its thickness from 50 to 75 feet (15 to 23 meters) and makes up the most fertile soil in Africa. It forms a plain that extends 100 miles (160 kilometers) from north to south, its greatest east–west extent being 155 miles (250 kilometers). The land surface slopes gently to the sea.

The fact that the Nile—unlike other great rivers known to them—flowed from the south northward and was in flood at the warmest time of the year was an unsolved mystery to the ancient Egyptians and Greeks. The mystery remained unsolved before the 20th century, except for early records of the river level that the ancient Egyptians made with the aid of nilometers (gauges formed by graduated scales cut in natural rocks or in stone walls), some of which still remain.

This prehistoric flaked flint hand axe was discovered along the lower Nile. SSPL via Getty Images

PREDYNASTIC EGYPT

Ages ago the land of Egypt was very different from what it is today. There was more rain. The plateau on each side of the Nile was grassland. The people wandered over the plateau in search of game and fresh pastures and had no permanent home. They hunted with a crude stone hand ax and with a bow and arrow. Their arrows were made of chipped flint.

Very gradually the rains decreased and the grasslands

dried up. The animals went down to the valley. The hunters followed them and settled at the edge of the jungle that lined the river.

In the Nile Valley the people's way of life underwent a great change. They settled down in more or less permanent homes and progressed from food gathering to food producing. They still hunted the elephant and hippopotamus and wild fowl, and they fished in the river. More and more, however, they relied for meat on the animals they bred— long-horned cattle, sheep, goats, and geese.

The early Egyptians learned that the vegetables and wild grain they gathered grew from seeds. When the Nile floodwater drained away, they dug up the ground with a wooden hoe, scattered seeds over the wet soil, and waited for the harvest. They cut the grain with a sharp-toothed flint sickle set in a straight wooden holder and then ground it between two flat millstones. The people raised emmer (wheat), barley, a few vegetables, and flax. From the grain they made bread and beer, and they spun and wove the flax for linen garments.

This wooden statue from Egypt's 5th dynasty (2416–2392 BC) shows a woman grinding grain. **Louisa Gouliamaki/AFP/Getty Images**

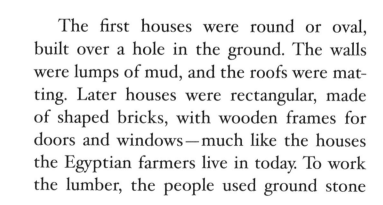

This mural of marshland birds comes from a tomb in ancient Thebes.
DEA/M. Carrieri/De Agostini/Getty Images

The first houses were round or oval, built over a hole in the ground. The walls were lumps of mud, and the roofs were matting. Later houses were rectangular, made of shaped bricks, with wooden frames for doors and windows—much like the houses the Egyptian farmers live in today. To work the lumber, the people used ground stone axheads and flint saws. Beautiful clay pottery was created, without the wheel, to hold food and drink. They fashioned ornaments of ivory, made beads and baskets, and carved figures of people and animals in stone. They built ships that had oars, and they carried on trade with nearby countries. Instead of names, the ships had simple signs, probably indicating the home port. These signs were an early step in the invention of writing.

IRRIGATION

As an aid to cultivation, irrigation almost certainly began in Egypt. The first use of the Nile for irrigation in Egypt began when seeds were sown in the mud left after the annual floodwater had subsided. With the passing of time, these practices were refined until a traditional method emerged, known as basin irrigation. Under this system, the fields on the flat floodplain were divided by earth banks into a series of large basins of varying size but some as large as 50,000 acres (20,000 hectares). During the annual Nile flood, the basins were flooded and the water allowed to remain on the fields for up to six weeks. The water was then permitted to drain away as the river level fell, and a thin deposit of

An Archimedes screw being used to irrigate crops on the Nile delta. The device works as a hydraulic screw to raise water from a lower level. **J.W. Thomas/Hulton Archive/Getty Images**

rich Nile silt was left on the land each year. Autumn and winter crops were then sown in the waterlogged soil. Under this system only one crop per year could be grown on the land, and the farmer was always at the mercy of annual fluctuations in the size of the flood.

Along the riverbanks and on land above flood level, some perennial irrigation was always possible where water could be lifted directly from the Nile or from irrigation channels by such traditional means as the *shadoof* (a counterbalanced lever device that uses a long pole); the *sakieh*, or Persian waterwheel; or the Archimedes screw.

In time they engaged in large-scale irrigation work, digging canals that cut across miles of land. This required the cooperation of many people living in different places. Leaders became necessary to plan the work and direct the workers. Because of this need, orderly government arose.

ON THE THRESHOLD OF HISTORY

Population and wealth grew with the increase in farmland. There was enough food to support a class who worked at crafts instead of farming. Villages grew into towns. Large towns spread their rule over nearby villages and became states.

At the end of the prehistoric period, there were only two political units—Lower Egypt (the delta) and Upper Egypt (the valley). Later, when Egypt was united, the people still called it the Two Lands, and the king of all Egypt wore a double crown combining the white crown of the south with the red crown of the north.

Before the prehistoric period ended, the Egyptians were stimulated by their contact with people who lived in the Mesopotamian river valley in what is now Iraq. These people were more advanced than the Egyptians in working metal, and they also had writing, although the Egyptians developed a very distinct script of their own. This great invention brought Egypt abruptly to the threshold of history, for history begins with written records.

This illustration shows a pharaoh wearing the double crown symbolizing the union of Upper and Lower Egypt. **Hulton Archive/Getty Images**

CHAPTER 2
THE DYNASTIES OF EGYPT

The beginnings of writing in Egypt go back to about 3100 BC, when the Two Lands became united in a single kingdom. According to tradition, it was Menes, a king of Upper Egypt, who brought about the union. He stands first in the long line of kings who ruled Egypt for about 3,000 years. Egyptian priests made lists of their kings, or pharaohs, and noted the most important events of their reigns. About 280 BC one of these priests, Manetho, grouped the pharaohs into 30 dynasties. (A dynasty is a succession of rulers of the same line of descent.)

Modern historians group the dynasties into periods. The periods when Egyptian civilization flourished are the Old Kingdom, the Middle Kingdom, and the New Kingdom. These are separated by periods of decline called the First Intermediate Period and the Second Intermediate Period. The final period of decline is called the Late Period.

The Great Sphinx at Giza, 4th dynasty. E. Streichan/Shostal
Associates

THE OLD KINGDOM

Little is known of Menes' successors until
the reign of King Zoser, or Djoser, at the end
of the 3rd dynasty. Zoser's capital was located
at Memphis, on the Nile's west bank near the
point where the Two Lands met. Imhotep, a
master builder, erected Zoser's tomb, the step

pyramid of Saqqara, on high ground over-looking the city. This monument—the first great building in the country made entirely of stone—marked the beginning of Egypt's most creative period, the Pyramid Age.

Later kings built their tombs in true pyra-midal form. Each pyramid guarded the body of one king, housed in a chamber deep within the pile. The climax of pyramid building was reached in the three gigantic tombs erected for Kings Khufu (Cheops), Khafre, and Menkure at Giza (Gizeh). Near them in the sand lies the Great Sphinx, a stone lion with the head of King Khafre.

The Old Kingdom lasted about 500 years. It was an active, optimistic age, an age of peace and splendor. Art reached a brilliant flow-ering. Sculpture achieved a grandeur never later attained. The pharaoh kept a splendid court. The people worshiped him as a god on Earth, for they believed him to be the son of Ra, or Re, the great sun-god. They called him *pr-'o* (in the Bible, pharaoh), meaning "great house."

A statue of Pharaoh Khafre. **Hulton Archive/ Getty Images**

THE PYRAMIDS OF GIZA

In the 26th century BC, as Egyptian civilization was reaching its height, three kings—Khufu, his son Khafre, and his grandson Menkure—ordered the construction of three huge pyramids that would serve as their tombs. The first of these, the Great Pyramid, is the largest

The three large pyramids of Menkure (left), Khafre (center), and Khufu loom over the horizon at Giza, just outside Cairo, Egypt. Sean Gallup/ Getty Images

ever built. It stands with the other two pyramids and the Great Sphinx in a cluster near the town of Giza. The ancient Greeks named the pyramids one of the Seven Wonders of the World, and today they are the only one of those wonders that still exists.

King Khufu's pyramid rests on a base that covers 13 acres (5.3 hectares), and each side of the base is about 756 feet (230 meters) long. The Great Pyramid once rose to a height of 481 feet (147 meters), but the top has been stripped. Originally 471 feet (143 meters) high, Khafre's pyramid was only 10 feet (3 meters) lower than his father's tomb. Menkure's pyramid, much smaller, rose to 218 feet (66 meters). Three small pyramids built for Khufu's queens stand near his pyramid. Also nearby are several temples and rectangular tombs built for other relatives and courtiers.

The Egyptian rulers ordered the pyramids to be built because they feared their remains would be disturbed by grave robbers. They chose a site on the west side of the Nile River because they believed that the home of the dead was toward the setting sun. The burial

chambers were placed under the exact centers of the pyramids. Passageways, which were built angling down from the sides and leading to the chambers, were later sealed with heavy stones. The pyramids did not achieve their purpose of protecting the ancient tombs, however. Over the centuries looters broke into most of them and stole the jewels and other treasures that had been buried in them.

The Greek historian Herodotus, writing 2,400 years ago, estimated that 100,000 men labored for 20 years to complete the Great Pyramid. It is also estimated that 2.3 million stone blocks were used to build the pyramid. Many authorities believe that the blocks of stone were moved up a circular ramp constructed around the pyramid as it was built up.

About 2200 BC the Old Kingdom came to an end. Nobles became independent and ruled as if they were kings. The country was split up into small warring states. Irrigation systems fell into disrepair. According to writers of the time: "The desert is spread throughout the land. The robbers are now in the possession of riches. Men sit in the bushes until the benighted traveler comes to . . . steal what is upon him." Thieves broke into the pyramids and robbed them of their treasures. The archaeologists of today can only imagine the treasures they might have unearthed had thieves not stolen them first.

THE MIDDLE KINGDOM

The Middle Kingdom period began about 2050 BC. After a long struggle, the rulers of Thebes won out over their enemies and once again united Egypt into a single state. Thebes was then a little town on the Nile in Upper Egypt. In the New Kingdom it became one of the ancient world's greatest capitals.

The pharaohs of the Middle Kingdom constructed enormous irrigation works in the Faiyum, a low-lying area west of the Nile. Noting the annual heights of the Nile flood at Aswan, they laid plans to use the Nile water wisely.

They sent trading ships up the Nile to Nubia in the south and across the sea to Mediterranean lands. They got gold from Nubia and copper from the mines in Sinai. Construction of the most colossal temple of all time, the Temple of Amen (Amon) at El Karnak, was begun.

After two centuries of peace and prosperity, Egypt entered another dark age. About

1800 BC it fell for the first time to foreign invaders. Down from the north came the Hyksos, a barbarian people who used horses and chariots in combat and also had superior bows. The Egyptians, fighting on foot, were no match for them. The Hyksos occupied Lower Egypt, living in fortified camps behind great earthen walls; but they failed to conquer Upper Egypt. When the Egyptians had learned the new methods of warfare, the ruler Kamose began a successful war of liberation.

THE NEW KINGDOM

A new era dawned for Egypt after the Hyksos had been expelled. This period, the New Kingdom, was the age of empire. The once-peaceful Egyptians, having learned new techniques of warfare, embarked on foreign conquest on a large scale. The empire reached its peak under Thutmose III, one of the first great generals in history. He fought many campaigns in Asia and extended Egypt's rule to the Euphrates.

Slaves and tribute poured into Egypt from the conquered nations. The tribute was paid in goods, for the ancient world still did not have money. Wall paintings show people

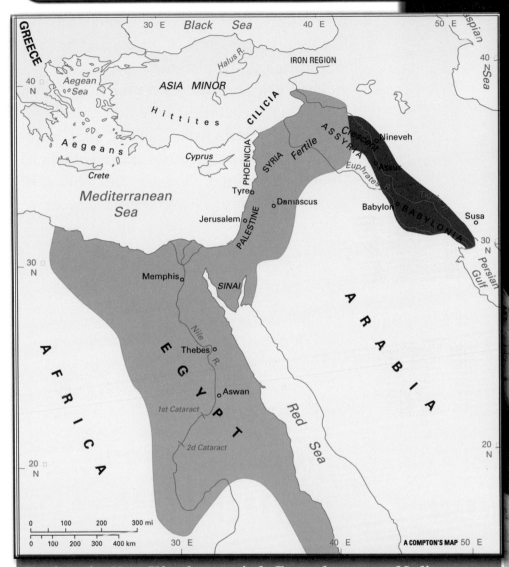

The following labels appear on the map:

GREECE

30 E Black Sea 40 E 50 E

Aspian Sea

40 N

Aegean Sea

ASIA MINOR

Halus R.

IRON REGION

40 N Sea

Hittites

CILICIA

ASSYRIA

Nineveh

Aegeans

Cyprus

PHOENICIA

SYRIA

Fertile

Crescent

Euphrates R.

Assur

Crete

Tyre

Damascus

Babylon

BABYLONIA

Susa

Mediterranean Sea

Jerusalem

PALESTINE

30 N

Memphis

SINAI

30 N Sea

Persian Gulf

A R A B I A

Nile R.

E G Y P T

Thebes

Aswan

1st Cataract

Red Sea

20 N

A F R I C A

20 N

2d Cataract

0 100 200 300 mi
0 100 200 300 400 km

30 E 40 E **A COMPTON'S MAP** 50 E

During the New Kingdom period, Egypt became a Mediterranean empire. Around 1479 BC Thutmose III, riding "in a chariot of fine gold," led his armies out of Egypt into Phoenicia, Palestine, and Syria. In later campaigns he extended the empire to the Euphrates Valley in Mesopotamia. Earlier rulers had already pushed the frontiers south into Nubia, beyond the First Cataract of the Nile.

37

from Nubia, Babylonia, Syria, and Palestine bearing presents on their backs and bowing humbly before the pharaoh.

The Egyptian rulers used their new wealth and slaves to repair the old temples and build new ones. Hatshepsut, Egypt's first great female leader, enlarged the great Temple of Amen at El Karnak. She also built her own beautiful temple at Deir el Bahri.

The temple of Queen Hatshepsut in Luxor, Egypt. Hatshepsut was one of the most powerful female monarchs of the ancient world. **Mladen Antonov/AFP/Getty Images**

Amenhotep III built the wonderful Temple at Luxor and put up the famous pair of colossal seated statues called the Colossi of Memnon. In the Middle Kingdom period, the pharaohs of Thebes had built modest brick pyramids for their tombs. In the New Kingdom period they broke with this tradition and began to hew tombs deep in the cliffs of an isolated valley west of Thebes. About 40 kings were buried in this Valley of the Tombs of the Kings.

In the last years of his reign Amenhotep III paid little attention to the empire. It was already decaying when his son Amenhotep IV came to the throne. This king was more interested in religion than in warfare. Even before his father's death, he began to promote a new religious doctrine. He wanted the people to give up all their old gods and worship only the radiant sun, which was then called Aten. He changed his name from Amenhotep ("Amen is satisfied") to Ikhnaton (Akhenaton; "It is well with Aten"). He left Thebes and built a splendid new capital sacred to Aten at El Amarna in middle Egypt. Throughout the land he had the word "gods" and the name "Amen" removed from tombs and monuments.

Ikhnaton's idea of a single god gained no hold on the Egyptian people. His successor, Tutankhamen, moved the capital back to Thebes and restored the name of Amen on monuments. Tutankhamen is famous chiefly for his lavishly furnished tomb, discovered in 1922. Its treasures reveal the luxury of the most magnificent period of Egyptian history.

Half a century later Ramses II completed the gigantic hall at El Karnak and set up many statues of himself. He also had his name carved on monuments built by earlier rulers, so that he became better known than any other king. He regained part of Egypt's Asian empire. But the kings who followed

The coffinette for the viscera (internal organs) of Tutankhamen. **Daniel Berehulak/ Getty Images**

him had to use the army to defend Egypt against invaders.

THE DECLINE OF EGYPTIAN POWER

In the Late Period, the final decline of Egypt's power set in. The treasury had been drained by extensive building projects and by the army. Hungry workers had to resort to strikes to get their wages in grain. The central government weakened, and the country split up once more into small states.

About 730 BC, Kushite invaders from the kingdom directly to the south entered Egypt and established a strong, new dynasty. However, they were unable to withstand an invasion from the north by the Assyrians. When Assyria's power waned, a new Egyptian dynasty reorganized the country. Persia conquered Egypt in 525 BC and held it until 404 BC. Three brief Egyptian dynasties followed, ending with the 30th, which fell to a second Persian conquest in 341 BC.

Persian rule lasted until the Macedonian conqueror Alexander the Great invaded Egypt in 332 BC. After Alexander's death, Ptolemy, one of his generals, seized the

Archaeologists restore a mosaic inside the rebuilt library in Alexandria, Egypt. The original Alexandria Library was founded in 295 BC and was the intellectual hub of the ancient world. **Norbert Schiller/Getty Images**

throne. The Ptolemys introduced Greek manners and ideas into Egypt. The city of Alexandria became the center of Greek civilization in the Near East. It was particularly famous for its extensive library.

The rule of Egypt by the Ptolemaic line ended with the beautiful Queen Cleopatra, who reigned first with her brother Ptolemy XIII, then with her brother Ptolemy XIV, and finally with Caesarion, her son by Julius Caesar. In 30 BC Egypt was proclaimed a province of Rome.

CLEOPATRA

One of the most fascinating women of all time was Cleopatra VII, queen of Egypt. She had great intelligence and beauty, and she used both to further Egypt's political aims.

Cleopatra was of Greek heritage and culture, one of the Ptolemy line set on the throne of Egypt after the conquest of Alexander the Great. Her father, Ptolemy XII, named her and his elder son, Ptolemy XIII, joint rulers. Cleopatra was around the age of 18 when she came to the throne in 51 BC. Three years later young Ptolemy's supporters had Cleopatra driven into exile. During this time, Rome had become a powerhouse. But it was under divided leadership.

In 48 BC the powerful Roman general Julius Caesar appeared in Egypt in pursuit of his rival, Pompey. When Cleopatra heard that Caesar was in the palace in Alexandria, she had one of her attendants carry her to him, rolled up in a rug offered as a gift. Captivated by her charm, the 52-year-old Roman helped her regain her throne. Ptolemy XIII was drowned, and Caesar made Cleopatra's younger brother, Ptolemy XIV, joint ruler with her.

Cleopatra bore Caesar a son, called Caesarion, meaning "little Caesar." When Caesar returned to Rome, she followed him with their baby and lived in Caesar's villa, where he visited her constantly. After Caesar was assassinated in 44 BC, Cleopatra returned to Egypt. Soon after, Ptolemy XIV died, perhaps poisoned by Cleopatra, and the queen named her son Caesarion co-ruler with her as Ptolemy Caesar.

Civil war followed Caesar's assassination, and the Roman Empire was divided. Mark Antony, as ruler of the eastern empire, summoned Cleopatra to Tarsus, in Asia Minor, to answer charges that she had aided his enemies. The queen arrived, dressed as Venus, on a magnificent river barge. Fascinated by her, Antony followed her to Alexandria.

The Roman fleet of Octavian clashes with the combined Roman-Egyptian fleet commanded by Mark Antony and Cleopatra in the battle of Actium. **MPI/Archive Photos/Getty Images**

After returning to Rome, Antony married Octavia, sister of Octavian (a powerful politician who later changed his name to Augustus and became Rome's first emperor), though he still loved Cleopatra, who had borne him twins. When he went east again, he sent for her and they were married.

Octavian was furious and declared war on Cleopatra. Antony and Cleopatra assembled 500 ships. Octavian blockaded them off the west coast of Greece, and the famous 31 BC battle of Actium followed. Cleopatra slipped through the blockade and Antony followed her, but his fleet surrendered.

The next year Octavian reached Alexandria and again defeated Antony. Cleopatra took refuge in the mausoleum she had had built for herself. Antony, informed that Cleopatra was dead, stabbed himself. Soon another messenger arrived, saying Cleopatra still lived. Antony insisted on being carried to her and died in her arms. Later Cleopatra committed suicide—tradition says by the bite of a poisonous snake called an asp.

After the Roman Empire was divided in half in the 4th century AD, Egypt was ruled from Constantinople by the Byzantine emperors. During this period most Egyptians were converted to Christianity. In the 7th century, Egypt fell to the Arabs.

CHAPTER 3
EVERYDAY LIFE IN ANCIENT EGYPT

People today live in an age when every year brings forth new inventions and discoveries, new fads and fashions that affect everyday life. Through communications, migration, and travel, foreign cultures merge into new lifestyles.

The Egyptians had their greatest creative period at the very beginning of their long history. After that, their way of living changed very little through the years. It is therefore possible to describe their homelife and their art without reference to the historical periods of Egyptian history.

Woman wearing sheathlike gown held up by shoulder straps, typical of Egyptian dress of the Old and Middle Kingdoms. Painted wood statue from the tomb of Meketre, Deir el Bahri, Egypt, 11th dynasty (2081–1938 BC); in the Egyptian Museum, Cairo. **Borromeo/Art Resource, New York**

UPPER-CLASS HOMELIFE AND DRESS

Egypt was protected by the sea on the north and by deserts to the east and west. For many centuries the Egyptians could develop their own way of life without fear of invasion by foreign armies. Their interests were centered in their homes and families and in their work. Their stone tombs were a kind of insurance against death. They loved life and wanted it to go on forever.

Villages and towns were situated near the Nile because it was the chief highway as well as the only source of water. Even the rich lived in houses of mud brick. The walls were richly colored. Windows were small, high openings covered with loosely woven matting to keep out the heat and glare of the sun. The most fashionable district was near the king's palace. Even here, houses were crowded close together to leave more space for farmland. Some dwellings were two stories high. Usually houses were built back to back to save space. Some opened onto a narrow street; others faced a small walled garden.

The walls were decorated with bright frescoes. Straw matting and rugs covered the floors. Lamps were saucers of oil with a floating wick. Rich people had beds, chairs, and stools but no real dining tables. They kept their clothes and linen sheets in box chests or in baskets. The linen was sent to professional laundrymen to be washed in the river.

The ancient Egyptians stored their water and food in huge pottery jars. To prepare foods, the cook used pottery bowls, placing

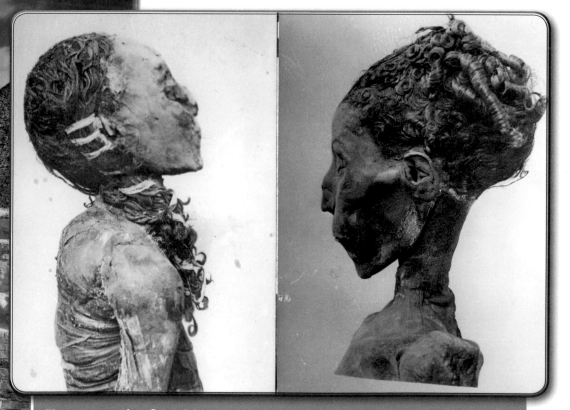

Two mummies found by archaeologists at Luxor, Egypt, with natural hair wigs on their heads. The mummies are estimated to be 4,000 years old. **Keystone/Hulton Archive/Getty Images**

them directly on the fire or in a clay oven. She baked bread and cake and roasted beef, mutton, goose, or wild fowl. The common drinks were beer, wine, and milk. Honey and dates were the only sweets. Almost everything the family needed was grown or made by workers belonging to the estate on which the family lived.

The members of Egypt's upper classes spent much of their time tending to their appearance. They bathed with soda instead of soap and then rubbed perfumed oil into the skin. Men shaved with a bronze razor. They cut their hair short and wore wigs. Women also wore wigs or added false braids to their own hair. They had combs and hairpins and mirrors of polished bronze or silver.

Both men and women darkened their eyelids with black or green paint. Women rouged their cheeks and lips and stained their nails with henna. The women usually kept their cosmetics in beautiful box chests.

Because of the hot climate, both men and women wore white linen clothes. Men usually wore only a skirt. In the early centuries the skirts were short and narrow; later they were long and full. Women wore low-cut white dresses with bands over the shoulders. Young children wore nothing at all.

FURNITURE OF THE ANCIENT EGYPTIANS

The furniture of the ruling class of ancient Egypt was richly ornamented and sophisticated, though houses were sparsely furnished by 20th-century standards. Much of this furniture has survived from the Egyptian custom of burying household objects in tombs where they were preserved until rediscovered by archaeologists in modern times. Other evidence is derived from pictorial sources.

The principal forms were the bed, the throne chair, small tables, stools, and boxes and small chests. The bed consisted of a simple, rectangular frame with short legs—often carved in the form of animal legs—that supported a framework of woven cord. Crescent-shaped headrests were used in place of pillows. Throne chairs, reserved for individuals of great importance, also often had legs and feet carved to resemble animal legs. Their square backs were inlaid with ebony and ivory, and their seats were of leather or woven cord. Small stools, some with crossed legs terminating in duck's heads, were common. Small boxes and chests were used for storing linen, clothing, and personal goods such as jewelry.

Decoration in gold and silver foil or leaf was not uncommon on the most expensive furniture, while less costly objects were painted in imitation of more valuable materials. Images used for decoration were often taken from Egyptian gods and other religious symbols. Inlay was usually applied in geometric or nearly abstract designs. While relatively simple furniture was used by most people, the furniture of Egypt's ruling class was very richly designed.

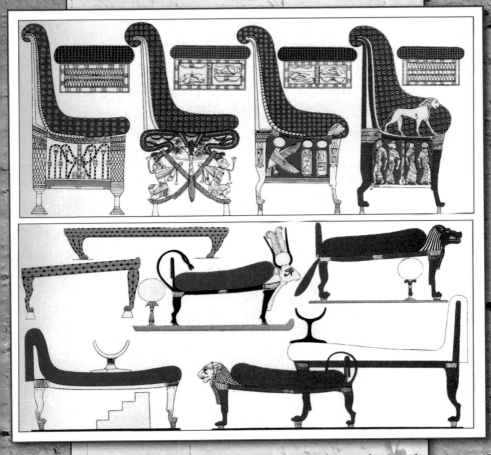

Illustration of Egyptian furniture - beds, couches, and thrones. Buyenlarge/Archive Photos/Getty Images

Both men and women wore jewelry—collars and necklaces, strings of beads, bracelets, anklets, earrings, and finger rings. Silver was more precious than gold.

PEASANTS AND CRAFTSMEN

The luxurious life of the pharaoh and the nobles was made possible by the continual labor of the peasants who tilled the soil. After the crops were harvested, the pharaoh could call on them to leave their village huts and go off to labor on irrigation works, to quarry stone with primitive tools, or to build tombs and temples. Their only pay was grain from the state granaries, oil, fish, vegetables, and clothing.

The craftsmen and artists worked in shops close to the palace of the pharaoh or on the estates of priests and nobles. Their professions were hereditary, passed down from father to son. An artist was never hurried. If he could produce a masterpiece, it did not matter whether he worked on it for one year or ten.

The highly skilled smiths forged bronze tools and weapons and made fine copper and bronze dishes for the homes of the rich Egyptians. Goldsmiths and silversmiths also made tableware as well as richly wrought

Mural painting of a farmer from an ancient Egyptian tomb. **DEA/G. Dagli Orti/De Agostini/Getty Images**

jewelry set with turquoise, carnelian, lapis lazuli, and other semiprecious stones and gems. Craftsmen in stone ground out vases, jars, bowls, and platters in hard diorite and porphyry or in soft, cream-colored alabaster, which could be ground so thin it let the light shine through.

The Many Uses of Papyrus

The ancient Egyptians made a kind of paper from the stalks of a reed called papyrus. This graceful plant, also called paper plant, grows from 4 to 15 feet (1 to 4.5 meters) tall in quietly

Close-up of a papyrus plant. **DEA/C. Sappa/De Agostini/Getty Images**

flowing water. Its green, jointless, bluntly triangular stems bear long, sharp leaves. Radiating flower clusters bloom at the tip of each stem. The Egyptians made a parchmentlike paper, also called papyrus, from the pith, or inner portion, of the stalk.

Papyrus stalks were also used to make boats and to weave baskets. The fiber provided materials for sails, matting, and rope. Caulk for boats was derived from the pith, and, when dried, the roots furnished fuel.

The scientific name of the papyrus plant is *Cyperus papyrus*. The plant is now cultivated chiefly as an ornamental in parts of northern and tropical Africa.

Potters turned clay vessels on a potter's wheel and then baked them in closed clay furnaces as tall as a man. They covered some of the pottery with a blue glaze. Women wove sheer fabrics of linen for clothing and for tapestries and awnings to decorate the houses of the rich.

Egypt then as now had little timber. Cedar and cypress were imported from Lebanon and tropical woods from Nubia. Cabinetmakers fashioned chairs and couches. Other craftsmen overlaid the furniture with precious metals or inlaid it with ebony or ivory.

The leatherworker contributed cushions. Shipbuilders made Nile vessels with curving hulls and tall sails and cargo ships to sail to foreign lands. Paperworkers took the papyrus reeds gathered from the Nile marshes, split them, and pasted them crosswise into double sheets of pale yellow writing paper.

SCRIBES

The introduction of writing in Egypt in the predynastic period (c. 3000 BC) brought with it the formation of a special class of literate professionals, the scribes. By virtue of their writing skills, the scribes took on all the duties of a civil service: record keeping, tax accounting, the management of public works (building projects and the like), even the prosecution of war through overseeing military supplies and payrolls. Young men enrolled in scribal schools to learn the essentials of the trade, which included not only reading and writing but also the basics of mathematics.

Some of what is known of Egyptian mathematics comes from two long papyrus documents that once served as textbooks within scribal schools. The Rhind papyrus (in the British Museum) is a copy made in the 17th century BC of a text two centuries older still. In it is found a long table of fractional parts to help with division, followed by the solutions of 84 specific problems in arithmetic and geometry. The Golenischchev papyrus (in the Moscow Museum of Fine Arts), dating from the 19th century BC, presents 25 problems of a similar type. These problems reflect well the functions the scribes would perform, for they deal with how to distribute beer and bread as wages, for example, and how to measure the areas of fields as well as the volumes of pyramids and other solids.

The most striking features of the Egyptian achievement in mathematics are competence and continuity. The scribes managed to work out the basic arithmetic and geometry necessary for their official duties as civil managers, and their methods persisted with little evident change for at least a millennium, perhaps two.

I n very early times each town had its own town-god as well as a number of lesser gods. There were also gods that everybody worshiped. The most important of these were Ra, the sun-god; Horus, the sky-god; and Osiris, the god of the dead.

When a town grew in influence, its town-god became more important, too. People worshiped him as part of their allegiance to the town. After Thebes became the capital, the worship of its town-god, Amen, spread throughout Egypt. The people combined his worship with that of Ra, and in this form called him Amen-Ra. Temples were raised to Amen throughout Egypt. The most splendid was the Temple at El Karnak, in Thebes.

THE STORY OF RA AND OSIRIS

The people believed that every day Ra, the sun, sailed across the sky in his boat. Every night he disappeared into the underworld, in the west. In the underworld, they thought, was another Nile River.

The Goddess Isis

Osiris's queen was Isis, who was also his sister. She represented the moon and was believed to have taught Egyptians the arts of agriculture and medicine. She was also credited with instituting marriage.

After Osiris was murdered by his evil brother, Seth, Isis recovered her husband's body, but Seth took it and cut it into pieces. Isis buried the pieces, and Osiris was thereafter

This mural painting of Anubis, Isis, and Osiris comes from the tomb of Nefertari in the Valley of the Queens in Luxor, Egypt. **De Agostini Picture Library/Getty Images**

regarded as god of the dead. His son, Horus, avenged the murder by conquering Seth.

Isis was frequently pictured with her infant son, Horus. She was also represented wearing cow's horns, since the cow was considered sacred to her. From the 7th century BC her cult was the most popular in Egypt. In the seaport of Alexandria she was regarded as patron of seafarers, and from there her worship spread to Greece and Rome.

Osiris, the ruler of the underworld, had the sun's boat pulled along this river until at last it crossed the horizon and the sun rose again.

Osiris had been murdered by his brother Seth but lived again in the underworld as king of the dead. The people looked to Osiris to give them, too, a life after death. Osiris was usually shown in human form, tightly swathed in linen like a mummy and wearing a high crown.

OTHER GODS AND SACRED ANIMALS

Other important deities were Nut and Hathor, goddesses of the sky and of joy;

A museum worker holds up a cat that was mummified in Egypt around 250 BC as an offering to the goddess Bastet. **William West/AFP/Getty Images**

Ptah, master artist and craftsman; Thoth, the moon-god, who was also scribe of the gods and the inventor of writing; and Khnemu, who fashioned men and women on a potter's wheel. Some gods, such as Amen and Osiris, were always represented in purely human form. Others were pictured as animals or with human bodies and animal heads. Thus Horus was worshiped in the form of a hawk, or falcon, or of a hawk-headed man. Thoth was an ibis, Khnemu was a ram, and Hathor was a cow. The sun had various symbols—the obelisk, the sacred scarab beetle, the uraeus cobra, and the sun disk.

Certain sacred animals were carefully kept in the temples. When Egyptian civilization decayed in its very late days, the people came to regard every animal of these species as sacred. They embalmed thousands of crocodiles, cats, and ibises and buried them in special cemeteries. Bulls were buried in stone vaults in an underground cemetery called the Serapeum, at Memphis.

ARCHITECTURE OF THE TEMPLES

Egyptian architecture was designed to blend into the setting of the Nile Valley, which is as level as a floor and is walled in on both

Visitors admire painted relief motifs in a chapel in the Opet Temple, part of the Karnak complex, in the ancient Egyptian city of Luxor. **Cris Bouroncle/AFP/Getty Images**

sides by sheer limestone cliffs. The temples erected by the Egyptians are gigantic; their surfaces, flat. The form is rectangular, like that of the flat-topped cliffs. The only decorations are reliefs and inscriptions that do not break the straight lines of the stone surfaces on which they are carved. Private tombs were decorated and inscribed in the same way.

Temples were built on a grand scale. The front wall consisted of two massive sloping towers, together called a pylon, with a door between them. The door gave entrance to a huge unroofed court, bordered on two or three sides by colonnades. Here the public assembled for worship. Beyond the court rose the hypostyle hall—a forest of huge pillars holding up a roof. Past the hall was the sanctuary of the temple-god. Only priests and the pharaoh were allowed to enter the sanctuary. There were many variations of this plan. Large temples—particularly the great Temple at El Karnak—had a series of courts, each faced by a pylon. An avenue of sphinxes led from El Karnak to the Temple at Luxor.

PAINTING AND SCULPTURE

Wall paintings took the place of reliefs in many private tombs of the New Kingdom. Some of the paintings and reliefs of this period rank with the world's finest masterpieces in art. In order to appreciate them, it is necessary to understand the principles upon which Egyptian artists worked.

Limestone ostracon with a drawing of a cat bringing a boy before a mouse magistrate, New Kingdom Egypt, 20th dynasty (1200–1085 BC); in the Oriental Institute, University of Chicago. **Courtesy of the Oriental Institute, University of Chicago**

Like other early peoples, the Egyptians did not use perspective. Figures at different distances from the observer were drawn in the same size. Humble people and servants, however, were pictured smaller than the great lord. Furthermore, the artist did not limit himself to a single point of view. He

drew what he knew, not merely what he saw. A fisherman in a boat might be sketched as if the artist were looking at the scene from the shore, but fish would be shown swimming under the water. The same picture might even outline the pond as if seen from above. Nevertheless, Egyptian paintings are beautiful and harmonious, and they reveal more than they would if drawn from a single point of view.

In sketching the human figure, the artist usually followed conventions established in early times. Since he wanted to show all the principal parts of the body, he combined front and side views. The head is always in profile, but the eye is drawn as it appears from the front. The shoulders and skirt are front view, but the legs and feet are side view.

Sculptors carved thousands of statues in all sizes, from colossal figures to miniatures. In addition to gods, kings, and nobles, their works included animals and sphinxes. The pharaoh is always shown in a dignified pose, never in movement. The face is often

A bust of Queen Nefertiti in the ancient Egypt collection at the Altes Museum in Berlin, Germany. **Sean Gallup/Getty Images**

an expressive portrait. The sculptor painted the bodies of men red and women pale yellow and set in eyeballs of colored stone or crystal.

THREE WAYS OF WRITING

The ancient Egyptians had three different ways of writing. They are called hieroglyphic, hieratic, and demotic. Hieroglyphs were chiseled on a stone surface. The word comes from two Greek words—*hieros*, meaning "sacred," and *glyphein*, meaning "to carve." From hieroglyphs the Egyptians developed a cursive writing. Called hieratic, this was written on papyrus with a pen. Out of hieratic a much more rapid script—demotic—developed in the Late Period.

Hieroglyphic writing developed out of picture writing toward the end of the prehistoric period. Picture recording evolved into writing with the realization that pictures could be used to express ideas if the words for these ideas had the same sounds as the names of the objects pictured. The picture of a house meant *house*; but it could also stand for the sound of the word for *house*, *pr*. The Egyptians did not write vowels. Because the word for *to go* also consisted of the consonants *pr* with a different vowel sound, the sign

The Rosetta Stone. Hulton Archive/Getty Images

for *house* could be used to write *to go* by adding to it a pair of walking legs. The legs sign—called a determinative—was not pronounced but indicated a verb of motion. Hieroglyphic writing was therefore sound writing. Some of the pictures stood for one consonant and were thus alphabetic, while others were used to represent two or three consonants.

In hieratic and demotic writing, the signs no longer resembled the pictures from which they were developed. Rapid cursive writing with a pen on the soft surface of papyrus led to shortening the signs.

The ability to read hieroglyphics died out with the Egyptian religion. Throughout the Middle Ages people thought the inscriptions on monuments were not writing but symbols with some deep religious meaning.

When Napoleon went to Egypt in 1798, he took with him a large staff of scholars and scientists to study the civilization of ancient Egypt. Near Rashid (Rosetta) one of his officers discovered a stone inscribed with three kinds of writing. Napoleon's scholars recognized the writing as Greek at the bottom, demotic in the middle, and hieroglyphic at the top. They could read the ancient Greek and guessed that the other sections must have the same content.

HIEROGLYPHICS

Ancient Egyptians had three different writing systems. The oldest, best known, and most difficult to read is called hieroglyphics. The word, which means "sacred carving," was used by Greeks who saw the script on temple walls and public monuments. The Greeks were somewhat mistaken in their terminology because hieroglyphs were used on gravestones, statues, coffins, vessels, implements, and for all sorts of nonreligious texts — songs, legal documents, and historical inscriptions.

Hieroglyphic writing has two main characteristics: objects are portrayed as ideograms or pictures, and the picture signs have the phonetic, or sound, value of the words represented by the objects. Thus hieroglyphs are not pictures only: they can be spoken, as are words written in an alphabet such as that of English. A written text normally contains three kinds of hieroglyphs: ideograms, which are read as the words they represent; phonograms, which are signs that do not refer to the objects they picture (they simply stand for one or more consonants); and determinatives, which have no phonetic value but help the reader to determine the correct meaning of the text.

Hieroglyphics were established as a writing system by at least 3100 BC. The system remained in use for about 3,500 years. The last known hieroglyphic inscription is dated AD 394. In the earliest period there were about 700 hieroglyphs. In this first stage of writing only the absolutely necessary symbols were invented. In the second stage of development easier readability was achieved by increasing the number of signs and by using determinatives. After the second stage, a period of about 2,000 years during which the system was essentially unaltered, the number of symbols increased to several thousand.

The stone fell into the hands of the British, who sent copies to scholars throughout the world. In 1822 Jean-François Champollion deciphered the hieroglyphs. Written about 196 BC, they commemorate the accession of Ptolemy V Epiphanes, about 205 BC. Champollion's work was the basis of the science of Egyptology—the archaeological study of pharaonic Egypt from the early beginnings of Egyptian culture to the Arab conquest in the 7th century.

Piece of papyrus with hieroglyphic inscription, Egyptian, 1400–1200 BC. This fragment of papyrus is from an Egyptian Book of the Dead. SSPL via Getty Images

THE LITERATURE OF ANCIENT EGYPT

Ancient Egyptian literature consists of both religious and nonreligious texts. The principal religious texts were designed to guide the dead into the underworld. In the Old Kingdom period such texts were written on the burial chamber walls in the pyramids of the 5th and 6th dynasties and are called Pyramid Texts. Later, "coffin texts" were written on the coffins of private citizens. Still later, religious texts—now called Book of the Dead—were written on papyrus rolls and buried with the dead. Nonreligious writings relate events in the lives of kings or citizens.

CONCLUSION

The civilization of ancient Egypt continues to hold a strong fascination for many people around the world, as the proliferation of documentaries and books about Egypt demonstrates. This interest has been fueled by a number of outstanding archaeological discoveries that have been made over the past century, including British archaeologist Howard Carter's discovery of the largely intact tomb of Tutankhamen in 1922 and French Egyptologist Pierre Montet's unearthing at Tanis of the tombs of kings from the 21st and 22nd dynasties in 1939–44.

The 1978 world tour of Tutankhamen artifacts heightened public fascination with ancient Egypt on a global scale. As increasing numbers of tourists visited Egypt, regional museums opened at Alexandria, Al-Minya, Mallawi, Luxor, and Aswan. In recent years, important new discoveries have been made that provide additional insight into the lives and culture of the ancient Egyptians. In the mid-1990s, for example, archaeologists found near Bawit, south of Cairo, one of the largest necropolises (burial places) ever uncovered; burials there dated to the Roman era, about 2,000 years ago. Excavators initially uncovered some 100 mummies, ranging from the remains of wealthy individuals buried with golden masks to those buried in less costly terra-cotta or plaster; workers dubbed the area the "Valley of the Golden Mummies," and experts believe that the necropolis may hold as many as 10,000 mummies.

In 2009–10 archaeologists made another important find with their discovery in Alexandria of the remains of a temple dedicated to Bastet, a goddess in the shape of a cat. Still, despite the decades of excavation and research that have been conducted, many sites remain in Egypt that have been only slightly explored, which only underscores the fact that there is much more yet to be learned about this eternally fascinating civilization.

asp A small venomous snake of Egypt similar to a cobra.

barge A roomy pleasure boat; especially a boat of state, elegantly furnished and decorated.

canopic jar A container in which the ancient Egyptians preserved the viscera of a deceased person usually for burial with the mummy.

deity A god or goddess.

demotic Of, relating to, or written in a simplified form of the ancient Egyptian hieratic writing.

dynasty A succession of rulers of the same line of descent.

embalm To treat a dead body so as to protect it from decay.

fresco A painting on freshly spread moist lime plaster with water-based pigments.

hieratic Constituting or belonging to a cursive form of ancient Egyptian writing simpler than the hieroglyphic.

hieroglyphic Written in, constituting, or belonging to a system of writing mainly in pictorial characters.

ibis A tropical or subtropical wading bird.

ideogram A picture or symbol used in a system of writing to represent a thing or an idea but not a particular word.

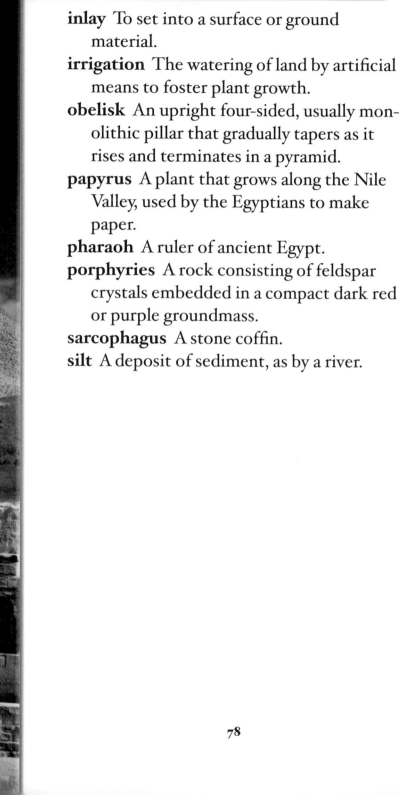

inlay To set into a surface or ground material.

irrigation The watering of land by artificial means to foster plant growth.

obelisk An upright four-sided, usually monolithic pillar that gradually tapers as it rises and terminates in a pyramid.

papyrus A plant that grows along the Nile Valley, used by the Egyptians to make paper.

pharaoh A ruler of ancient Egypt.

porphyries A rock consisting of feldspar crystals embedded in a compact dark red or purple groundmass.

sarcophagus A stone coffin.

silt A deposit of sediment, as by a river.

The American Research Center in Egypt
2 Midan Simon Bolivar
Garden City, Cairo 11461
Egypt
Web site: http://www.arce.org
The American Research Center in Egypt
   is active in working with the Egyptian
   Ministry of Culture to help preserve the
   heritage and culture of ancient Egypt.
   It is a private, nonprofit organization
   founded in 1948.

The British Museum
Ancient Egypt Department
Great Russell Street
City of London WC1B 3DG
United Kingdom
Web site: http://www.ancientegypt.co.uk
The British Museum houses an unparal-
   leled collection of artifacts from ancient
   Egypt. One of the keys to unlocking the
   secrets of hieroglyphics, the Rosetta
   Stone, is on display there.

Canadian Museum of Civilizations
Mysteries of Egypt
100 Laurier Street
Gatineau, QC K1A 0M8
Canada

(819) 776-7000
Web site: http://www.civilization.ca
This leading Canadian museum focuses pri-
marily on the history and culture of the
peoples of Canada. However, it also has a
fascinating online exhibition devoted to
increasing knowledge of the civilization
of ancient Egypt.

Metropolitan Museum of Art
Egyptian Art Department
1000 Fifth Ave
New York, NY 10028
(212) 535-7710
Web site: http://www.metmuseum.org/
works_of_art/egyptian_art
The Metropolitan Museum of Art has a
large collection of art and artifacts from
ancient Egypt. There is an extensive,
permanent exhibit on display in this New
York City museum.

Society for the Study of Egyptian Antiquity
3008 Utah Drive NW
Calgary, AB T2N 4A1
Canada
(403) 282-2153
Web site: http://www.thessea.org
With four chapters in Canadian

cities—Toronto, Montreal, Vancouver, and Calgary—the Society for the Study of Egyptian Antiquities is a nonprofit organization founded to stimulate interest in Egyptology.

WEB SITES

Due to the changing nature of Internet links, Rosen Educational Services has developed an online list of Web sites related to the subject of this book. This site is updated regularly. Please use this link to access the list:

http://www.rosenlinks.com/ancv/egyp

BIBLIOGRAPHY

Campbell-Hinshaw, Kelly. *Ancient Egypt* (Chronicle Books, 2007).

Chrisp, Peter. *Ancient Egypt Revealed* (DK Publishing, 2002).

Meltzer, Milton. *In the Days of the Pharaohs: A Look at Ancient Egypt* (Franklin Watts, 2001).

Perl, Lila. *The Ancient Egyptians* (Franklin Watts, 2004).

Ray, John *The Rosetta Stone and the Rebirth of Ancient Egypt* (Harvard Univ. Press, 2007).

Romer, John. *The Great Pyramid: Ancient Egypt Revisited* (Cambridge Univ. Press, 2007).

Sands, Emily. *The Egyptology Handbook: A Course in the Wonders of Egypt* (Candlewick Press, 2005).

Schomp, Virginia. *The Ancient Egyptians* (Marshall Cavendish Benchmark, 2008).

Steele, Philip. *Ancient Egypt* (Rosen Publishing, 2009).

Wilkinson, Richard H. *The Complete Temples of Ancient Egypt* (Thames & Hudson, 2000).

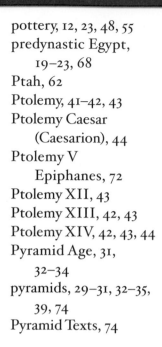